Addiction Demystified

Copyright Sofia Bothwell 2019 All Rights Reserved

ISBN 978-0-244-77671-8

No part of this book may be copied printed by electronic or any other means without prior permission from the author Sofia Bothwell. No part of this book is to be taken as medical advice. Sofia Bothwell is not liable for any result of the use of this material.

Addiction Demystified

This is the story of my own journey through several addictions. It starts when I was a teenager. A teenager who was craving. Craving food when full. A teenager who was obsessing, obsessing about size, shape and eating habits. During that journey of five years I learned about addiction, I learned about it through experience. Binge eating was my main addiction. I had no control nor ability to stop when physically full when I was on a binge. The rest of the time I was simply in a love/hate relationship with food, and constantly desiring my body to be slimmer. I can see now it was in a subconscious attempt to be accepted, to be loved, to be heard, to be appreciated. Of course *all that* was not going to happen just as the result of my being slimmer. The appreciation, protection and nurturing I would have liked, was not going to come from my family, nor from the school system either. Glimmers of it came through friends but not enough to really heal what was going on. And finding out, what was really going on, would unravel itself in a lifetime of healing. That lifetime of healing really started at the age of nineteen, when, on my lunch hour, I browsed the local bookstore in search of the latest diet that would be my answer, but somewhere in my consciousness already was dawning the stark realisation that dieting was not the answer. If it was, the last five years would not have escalated into the negative cycle of starving, binge eating and bulimia. Something was telling me that my eating habits were severely dysfunctional and that my attempts at dieting had only served to fuel the flames of that dysfunction. So miraculously out of that darkness, in an ordinary lunch hour, the light of a book touched me, and it was to change my life forever. That book was Fat Is A Feminist Issue by Susie Orbach.

In it I learned that, yes, what I suspected was true – Dieting was not the answer that would heal my problem. Giving up dieting was to be my first step. Then it taught me more, it gave me the missing information that would heal my problem. It taught me that I had unresolved emotional issues. It taught me what an emotional issue was. It taught me how we suppress our unresolved emotional issues through the act of eating when full. It taught me that eating when full is a way to cope with the emotional stuff that we are either not aware of, or simply want to numb ourselves to. It taught me that we all have unresolved emotional issues. It taught me that when we stop eating when full 100% of the time that our unresolved emotional issues surface. That means we feel the pain, fear, anger and boredom or stress that we previously avoided by eating when full. It taught me that the act of suppressing emotional issues is the act of addiction, in other words, I was addicted to eating *food when full* because that *food when full* enabled me to stay clear of my difficult emotional stuff. It taught me how we are conditioned to eat when full by well-meaning parents. It taught me that I could learn to give myself a positive outlook on life. It taught me I could break free from the madness of *eating when full* and the resultant weight gain forever. It taught me to resolve that previously unresolved emotional stuff. It taught me how to avoid binge eating by being aware of the underlying emotional issue that was surfacing and be able to meet it, and feel the uncomfortable feeling, and ask myself – Given the fact I feel this way, what would I like to do now?

Thus, it taught me how to tap into my own intuitive guidance and inner knowing on how to resolve my emotional issues. It gave me freedom. It gave me my road map out of addiction to food when full.

My life grew richer as a result. My life grew in awareness and understanding, and that awareness and understanding led me to leave home and move in with my boyfriend, and then, after six months, to emigrate to London, where I lived and worked and experienced the new. But addiction is a sly and insidious creature that snuck up on me when a difficulty struck. I did not know how to deal with the pain in my heart. London can be a cold and lonely place sometimes and my boyfriend turned out to be a lover of drink and pot. When I lived with him I was a non-smoker, but constantly inhaling secondary smoke was hard. Also his moods were erratic, his behaviour was difficult. He behaved like a demanding, overbearing idiot at times. And it frightened me.

What behaviour had been brought on by indulging in pot behind my back, and what was his own way of wounded relating (which in hindsight was narcissistic) I did not know. Again, I did not have the tools to cope with this new and strange situation, simply getting on with my own life and after about two years working in catering, I decided to better myself and take some evening classes and then a full time Art Class. The fact that he punched me the day before my interview at art school was bewildering to me. Now I realise it was the behaviour of a control freak. I did not have the emotional capacity to leave. I kept wishing and hoping he'd change (a sure sign of co-dependency). Three years later he still had not changed but somehow, I managed to leave. I rented a room in a shared house in North London. And a friend gave me the book 'Women Who Love Too Much' by Robin Norwood. Again, a book was to change my life.

In it I learned how we can be addicted to another person. Your focus on the other person serves as a distraction from your own pain and unresolved issues. You crave the other like a drug. Even though they mis treat you, you crave being with them and the idea of not being with them is unthinkable. The other may be married or an addict, or abusive to you physically or emotionally. Overbearing, critical, needy and selfish. They may be nice some of the time but often ignore you, your wants and needs, in subtle or overt ways. They could be manipulative, subtly aggressive, or in unspoken ways suggesting your course of action, choice of clothes, friends or work for example.

I was overjoyed to have the information and healing tools I had been praying for. I joined a self-help support group for other co-dependent women, and, as a recovered compulsive eater I started to research setting up my own workshops for eating disorder recovery. I approached the Womens' Therapy Centre in North London, and was invited to sit in on a nine-month support group for compulsive eating women with a view to set up my own support groups the following year. Which I did.

What is Addiction?

Mainstream ideas of addiction are slightly inaccurate. They usually oversimplify it to mean anything you do repeatedly and feels good. The truth is that addiction *can* be something that you do repeatedly and feels good, such as drinking alcohol. But look a little deeper, does that *feeling good* extend to the hangover? And is it helping you feel your feelings, resolve your issues or numb them? Many healthy things, in fact most healthy things can be defined as something you do repeatedly and feels good. Walking your dog for example feels good and you do it repeatedly. For me personally eating salad is something I do repeatedly and feels good. It is not an addiction because I stop when full.

What makes any activity an addiction, is one main thing – **It helps you to run away from your emotions.** So, if you think something is an addiction, ask yourself - Is this numbing me to my uncomfortable feelings and emotions? Is it enabling me to run away from a particular emotional dilemma that is currently bothering me?

- Addiction is anything that suppresses your emotions.
- Addiction is anything that momentarily helps you *feel better* but in the long run is detrimental.
- Addiction is usually *too much* – too much food, too much alcohol, too much work, too much spending.
- Addiction is the false coin accepted in exchange for your authentic life and resolving of emotional issues.
- Addiction is anything that distances you from your concerns.
- Addiction is what we try to fill the emotional gaps with.

Addiction Demystified

- Addiction is socially acceptable in the forms of *food when full,* alcohol, cigarettes and prescription drugs.
- Addiction is not socially acceptable in the form of illegal drugs.
- Addiction is a problem in itself, and, it is the symptom of a deeper problem. The deeper problem is an unresolved emotional issue or trauma. Resolve the deeper problem and the symptom clears up.
- Being an addict can also mean you have difficulty acting on your own behalf.
- An addict does not really take proper care of themselves. They may try fooling themselves and you, but snorting coke is not self-nurturing.

Where it comes from

The repetition of the cycle is insidious, and it starts in childhood and our family. How our mother treated us. How our father related to us. How our siblings related to us. The patterns are set. The wounds are accumulated. And the extent to which we are able to deal with our traumas, bumps and bruises, both the emotional and physical, will in no uncertain terms be the stuff that shapes our lives – all our life.

Yes, it all starts in childhood, except for the bits concerning when you were in the womb. Seriously, how your mother was feeling during the pregnancy can have a huge effect on you. Were you a wanted baby? Were your parents happy when your mother was carrying you in the womb? Was she feeling neglected, overwhelmed, sad or lost while carrying you? You absorbed her emotions in those nine months and they imprint on your life. If she herself was drinking, smoking, overeating or using drugs it all imprints on the embryo. Also, traumas from past lives may indeed play out in this lifetime in order to be resolved. Whether you believe in reincarnation or not, the truth is that if you died in a fire in the eighteenth century then you may have skin problems today. If you were persecuted in a former life or enslaved, or beheaded, the effects upon your feelings of injustice, or difficulty with authority figures such as your boss, or the rules of society, may be clouded by that unresolved trauma. Our lives in the vast cosmos of existence are fascinating and we can heal as we delve into, and resolve, through Rebirthing Breathwork or QHHT Quantum Healing Hypnosis Technique for example, the issues entailed and accumulated in the living of that mystery.

Rebirthing breathwork for me personally was a technique that I have been fascinated and enamored with since I first heard of the concept at the 'Women Who Love Too Much' Support Group I was attending at the age of 26. I immediately availed of the three discount sessions that the therapist was offering. I was amazed at the healing power of the breath. The ability to tap into the previously locked emotions and safely and healthily experience and release them in the session under the care of the Rebirthing Coach. The proof of the breathwork pudding was certainly after the sessions when I felt the shackles and chains of my addiction to my ex-boyfriend fall away, as I no longer craved his company, and was able to end all contact once and for all, and continue on my healing journey of self-nurturing and personal growth.

So, addiction basically comes from unresolved emotional issues and the fact that we feel we have no other way of coping with those emotions or traumatic events and their memories than to indulge in the addiction.

- Addiction is our band aid.
- We don't feel like we know of any other thing to do.
- We feel like we do not want to confront the emotional issue.
- We don't want to explore other ways of dealing with the emotions or traumas we suspect are lurking in the withdrawal symptoms.

- We want the 'comfort', the distraction that indulging in addiction brings. Meanwhile our life gets worse and worse.
- Or we are totally unaware of our pain and unresolved issues and therefore do not think our 'liking' drugs, cigarettes, food when full, or alcohol has anything to do with the suppression of emotion.
- We do not see the point in delving into, healing and feeling our emotions or traumas.
- We do not want to join AA or NA or a support group.
- We do not want to read a book on recovery.
- We actually do not even think there is a problem other than the problem of not being able to get a 'fix' whenever and wherever we want.

But that all changes when we hit our own personal rock bottom, and realise that indulging in the addiction is not working, and we start, to want, to heal. A rock bottom could be anything. For me it was being face down in the gutter after a binge on drink when a boyfriend did not show up. I never drank after that. That was over twenty years ago.

We join AA, or read the book, or join the support group, talk to other recovered addicts. Read the non-diet books, such as my books True Slimness, or Simply Full and Guidelines for Healing Your Eating Habit all by me Sofia Bothwell and available from Amazon or eBay.

The only thing that has the power to make you an addict is an unresolved emotional issue. Resolve your emotional issues and you heal your tendency towards addiction. It is a journey, a journey of feeling your feelings, being aware of your emotional stuff and being actively involved in dealing with it, making peace with it, otherwise known as - resolving it.

The methods and ideas outlined throughout this book help, but the main one is - Asking yourself, every time you have a craving: **What feeling is this?** And then –

Given the fact I feel this way what would I like to do now? Or - **How can I heal this?** If the answer is a healthy one, then get busy doing it. The answer comes from within. Only you know how to deal with the terror of being homeless. Only you know how to deal with waking up to the fact that your boyfriend is abusive to you and you need to leave him. Only you know how to deal with the feeling of abandonment at never having known your father, or having had an emotionally unavailable, critical father and a mother who wanted you to look after her even though you were only seven. Only you know how to deal with a situation of lack of education and a minimum wage job. Just to dismiss all these scenarios as hopeless is ineffective and quite frankly giving up too soon. Only when you tap into your intuition or gut instinct, will you be shown the way out. The whisper might be anything: For example: Get a job at that restaurant for the summer. Re-apply for that counselling course. Join AA. Speak to that neighbor that is always so friendly. Have the baby, say no to the abortion your boyfriend hinted at. Do not marry that guy. Go to that dance class. Spend a year doing overtime and save £300 a month for the deposit on a flat. Move house. Visit that city. Check out that group of like mined souls. Read that book. See that therapist your friend suggested.

The intuitive nudge can come in the form of a feeling or a thought, and is usually exciting and joyous. Finally go for what you would love to do, be and have. For example: If you love drawing join an Art Class.

Obviously do not follow thoughts or feelings to harm another but rather see them as a sign that further healing needs to be done because of your hatred or fear around that person. Forgiveness affirmations or beating pillows for anger towards another is useful in the healing of any strong emotions like that. Annalee Skarin's Prayer 'In the House of My Enemies' is very powerful to help you heal the suffering caused to you by others, and is on the Internet, you can Google it.

Addiction Demystified

The people who hurt you were literally your enemies and forgiving them enables you to heal. Remember forgiveness does NOT condone what they did – it heals you from what they did. That is a little-known truth about the power of forgiveness.

Forgiveness heals <u>you</u> from what they did.

Also check out Howard Wills on the Internet and his Concise Prayer Program for healing yourself.

Here is one of his prayers: Repeat daily 'God please help me forgive all people. All people forgive me. Help us all forgive ourselves. Please God, Thankyou God Amen.' You can use the word 'Love' or 'Source' instead of 'God' if you want. It preforms an inner cleansing of the ill effects of any traumas you suffered. It is like you become the person to whom no injustice or trauma ever happened. You are free of it and it's ill effects in your life.

Addiction is a symptom

Addiction is a symptom of a deeper problem. Whenever you look at someone (or observe yourself) drinking, smoking or carrying extra weight then you know the covert statement is: 'Hey, there is a problem here! And guess what, it is not just this extra weight I am carrying, or the cigarette I am smoking, or the 10th drink I am downing! This is just something I do to numb the pain.'

The pain is the root cause of the addiction. Heal the pain – heal the addiction.

The question is – Are you aware that there is pain you are numbing with the food when full, drink and cigarettes or through staying in an abusive relationship?

The next question is – Are you willing to contact that pain, acknowledge that pain, feel that pain, so you can ultimately heal that pain?

Are you willing to cease indulging in the food when full, drinking and/or smoking? Are you willing to leave that relationship, to feel that pain, get to know that emotional issue, in order to resolve it?

For it is in the 'getting to know' and resolving this emotional stuff that we break free from addiction. With every chunk of emotional debris resolved, a chunk of craving disappears and never returns. That is the real freedom – freedom from cravings!

How it affects you: It obviously affects how you are in the world when you grow up feeling unwanted, unloved, not heard nor listened to. If you were slapped, beaten or yelled at, it affects you. A Rebirthing Breathwork teacher of mine once said 'Most of us, as children were touched too roughly and/or too seductively.' That alone is a trauma. It is devastating and causes people to not really be able to function in their own best interests, because the pain, wherever it came from, does indeed cripple. So, we are left with a choice: To either suppress the pain through addictions or feel the pain and heal. AA is a good solution for many an alcoholic or drug addict. The stunning array of self-help books and alternative healing methods from Acupuncture to Zen Philosophy can all help and be part of your healing journey. It is up to you to tap into and follow that still small voice within that can be your guiding star throughout your life of recovery not victimhood.

There is another choice, and that is Behavior Problems such as The Narcissist that can evolve as a coping mechanism to suppress your pain so deeply that you never feel it, but become expert at dumping it. You may have had a Narcissistic parent and been subject to their cruelty but deeming it normal. Many a tyrannical boss, co-worker, parent, friend, sibling or spouse may display this trait and it is good to be aware of its characteristics so you can distance yourself from them. Or if you notice you yourself have this trait then you can self-heal.

Unreasonable, greedy, kill or be killed attitudes and behaviour are to be avoided when you see them in others, and healed if you see them in yourself.

Addiction Demystified

Manipulation and control tactics, overt or subtle, are the minefield that we live in when we are in relationship with a narcissist, but once we know its location, we can stay well away, and move towards healthy, happy friendships and relationships.

Awareness, awareness, awareness is a huge benefit to you. Awareness of your own patterns and behaviour, actions and reactions, emotions and feelings, likes and dislikes, problems and dilemmas. Awareness of the healing tools that can help you. Awareness of the dysfunctional patterns in others and the effect they have on you if you are around them, be they family members or not.

Knowledge and info from other recovered addicts is invaluable and again books and You Tube can be a great resource for this kind of life-changing knowledge.

Finances: If you feel worthless, it is going to affect your finances. If you are indulging in any addiction you may not be aware you feel worthless.

Sofia Bothwell

The issue of lack of finances has, pretty much, been a constant in my life. I've always had enough certainly, and I have usually been able to accomplish what I wanted. I've been on minimum wage and had a career that though I loved, only paid a small income, supplemented by my partners work when I was first a Mother with a small child to raise. But this left me financially dependent on the man – a situation I did not like. But again and again I was brought back to why I could not attain my financial goals. I saw parallels with the fat / slim dilemma here in the rich/poor dilemma. Were there deeper forces at play that were eluding me? I desired to be rich like I used to desire to be slim. It was the seemingly unattainable goal. It was the thing that would make everything alright. Common enough thinking within society. However, society is an addict.

One morning many years later, my child an independent adult by then; I was cycling home after doing a ten hour night shift as an industrial cleaner, I felt sick, nauseous. I thought – Is there elements of addiction here? Is this the 'hangover'? Is my *paycheck* the equivalent to the drunken high? I do feel I have no other way to make a living, at the moment, other than to do this very, very hard work that is literally exhausting me and making me sick? That is another hallmark of addiction – the feeling of *no choice*. Ok, so what is it I am running away from? I asked myself. What emotions would come up if I were not working so hard? Helplessness and hopelessness came to mind. Ok, so that is what I need to heal. The helpless, hopeless feelings to name a few. And I knew the tool to help me dislodge and heal that negative concept that I am helpless and hopeless – The Work of Byron Katie. So, I got to work and did The Work on my negative thoughts around finances and my career. I also knew I had to give up coffee because it was making me feel nauseous. And I started to feel more hopeful about my career while accepting that it was non existent at that time. I started to 'help myself' or 'act on my own behalf' concerning my career and busied myself writing and editing my manuscripts – the lifelong work I have done that although only earned me little or nothing, still, I felt to be one of the very reasons for my existence. I also felt writing to be part and parcel my authentic life. The creativity that was the real Mc Coy, without which, I would surely be really in the clutches of addiction again. So, I still worked as an industrial cleaner to keep a roof over my head, I did overtime to save for a house down-payment, and I continued to write and edit with a view to approaching agents and publishers. I actively started planning to set up a support group locally for compulsive eating women. In other words, I was planning my future and being creative while being in contact with and healing my emotional stuff. I used chanting to unearth and heal some deep-seated sorrows. I had learned the skill of Rebirthing Breathwork years ago so I rebirthed myself during this time through this breathwork meditation. Thus, I was staying clear of addiction, and the coffee cravings diminished; they were being replaced by an authentic, fulfilling life, even in the midst of physically and emotionally demanding a times. Then, I stopped doing overtime and this eliminated much of the grueling or self-punishment aspect of my work. I visited London more often, thus following my bliss, as I loved the place. There I distributed my flyers for my Weight Loss Skype Consultations and my self-published books. I got my books on Amazon. All positive steps that were part and parcel of healing the addiction to hard work that had been adversely affecting my health.

We become aware you see, aware of when there is potential for slipping back into addiction. We become aware of our feelings. We become aware of any cravings. Even if it is just craving coffee – we still know it is hiding some unresolved emotional issue that needs to be addressed in healthier ways, not suppressed. We don't compromise, we don't suppress – we heal. We have at our disposal the healing tools and we use them. We catch it early, and heal, and stay healed through self-awareness.

In this way, being aware of what elements of addiction could be lurking around in some part of your life, you are able to be one step ahead of it. You can minimize or delete it from your life. Being aware of our own feelings and resolving them; and being creative, brings the healing growing dynamic that obliterates addiction from our lives. I was being creative by writing. Whether I got paid for it or not was a side issue. I had to write to fill the emotional need to write. Each person's emotional needs are different, and you have to find yours in order to fill those needs, not suppress them through addiction. And you can discover what emotional needs you have by asking yourself – What would I love to do? For it is this *moving into our own authentic life* that seals the deal – freedom from addiction is ours.

Homelessness

How can we be homeless? Lack of money. The necessity to earn money to put a roof over our heads is prevalent in today's society run by banks and building regulations that practically make it illegal to build a shelter. But never mind the negative outlook and become aware of your own creative ability to provide shelter for yourself and your family if you have one. Staying with friends or family members is not always easy or wise especially if that family was the one that was the inflictor of the physical, sexual and/or emotional traumas you are healing. A job in McDonalds may just be the temporary answer that will bring you the cosy little home you desire even if it is a one roomed apartment or a flat share with a friend in recovery.

Staying away from the drink and drugs is easier when you are around people who do not drink or smoke. Have a place that you feel is peaceful and is supportive for the life you are building for yourself. Maybe £50 a month is spent on a therapy session. Reading, or listening to inspirational and informative videos on You Tube such as Russell Brand (recovered from drink and drug abuse) are wonderful resources to accompany you on your journey of a wonderful life. As the film title 'It's a Wonderful Life' you truly can have a wonderful life and a life filled with wonder as you progress, following your own inner pull towards that which you are interested in. So, what do you love to do? Who do you love to listen to? What is your dream life?

Drink and drugs

The warm afterglow of the vodka the clink of the ice in the glass, the fizzy sweetness of the Cola, all sipped by the pretty, slim, twenty-two-year-old with a lifetime of baggage that even she was not aware of. The numbing process had begun. A heartache of a betrayal had left sobriety to be not very welcome, and the hold of the alcohol and the cigarettes, topped up with accepting the joint as it was passed to her, clinched the deal – The pact made with addiction, saying, it would rule her life for another year or so. I was that twenty-two-year-old.

Now, all was not as dark as it seemed. I had already given up *eating when full*. I had already learned a bit about addiction and its dynamics. And I knew that the vodka and ciggies were a band aid for my broken heart. I was also aware that the current betrayal had probably brought to light all the other betrayals that lay hidden in my psyche. I was aware that I did not seem to have to tools to cope with this ever-present pain in my heart. Numbing it, seemed to be the best policy, but I knew without a shadow of a doubt I would conquer it. I didn't know how, but it would come to me, *the way out* would come to me. I did not know how to handle my boyfriend, so when a room became available in the huge house we had a bedsit in, I suggested he take it, and my friend who was coming over from Ireland stay with me in the double bedsit, until we worked things out. He agreed. That alone didn't heal my heartache, it seemed to worsen it. The darkness of those days was lit occasionally by a glimmer of positivity or pleasant feelings which were to be my saving grace and goodness knows how, but continued to pull me through, to a greater light and an addiction-free lifestyle. But it took time and the only tool I had, was to ask repeatedly – What is it that will heal this?

The Answer: As Chris Griscom author of Time is an Illusion, says, 'Use life' or in more old-fashioned terms – *If life gives you lemons, then make lemonade.* We all grasp the concept – *It's how you play the cards you are dealt*, but let's evolve that saying into what Michael Bernard Beckwith has stated: 'You can start with nothing and out of nothing and out of no way, a way will be made.' (Michael is a former drug dealer turned spiritual icon, founder of Agape International Healing Centre and author of several self-help books including The Answer Is You).

Emotions: That emotional soup in which lies the positive and negative, the joyous and the painful. It is in learning how to be emotional beings, how to process our emotions, how to feel our feelings that lies our freedom from addictions – all addictions.

How do I deal with my anger? Walk away from the person I am angry with and start to create my own life. Join a Yoga Class if you are drawn to Yoga. Join an Art Class if you love art. This is how you create your life, this is what being creative means – it is not rocket science. However, if you are drawn to rocket science by all means study Physics. Give yourself permission. Allow yourself to believe there is a way to have the life you would love to live – a life without drug highs or gorging uncontrollably on food when you are full and then feeling awful about your behavior. Self-control is only gained through self-compassion, self-understanding and self-forgiveness. Practice them all as best you can, and the healing comes.

As each individual changes from an addict to someone who is free from addiction, we enter a world where creativity and healing is the norm, where co-operation and interdependence is accepted and lived, where all our needs are met, where we all feel nurtured and loved, feel a sense of community and belonging. Where life is interesting, and funny, and everyone knows they are loved and appreciated for just being alive – all are precious beyond measure yet humble and happy. A life feeling fulfilled, a society of individuals existing in peace and a sobriety that stems from within and is a delight to participate in. Learning and growing all the time, and never yearning, nor wanting, nor craving, for all is satisfied, all is resolved, all is creativity.

About the Author:

Sofia Bothwell was born in Ireland to an upper middle-class Protestant family. With her Catholic boyfriend she emigrated to London at the age of twenty. After working in catering for a couple of years she embarked on independent study of addiction recovery, culminating in establishing self-help support groups for compulsive eaters. She trained as a Breath-work Coach in Italy. She has actively been involved in Home Education and the natural care of horses. She has written several books including self-help books, her biography and four novels all available from LULU the on line publishing company, Amazon and eBay. She currently resides in her Beloved Wales.

Addiction Demystified

Email: sofia2227@gmail.co.uk

Facebook: Sofia Bothwell or True Slimness

You Tube Channel: Sofia Bothwell

Web site: www.trueslimness.co.uk